DATE DUE

© Aladdin Books 1990

First published in
the United States in 1990 by
Gloucester Press Inc
387 Park Avenue South
New York NY 10016

Design: Rob Hillier, Andy Wilkinson
Editor: Catherine Bradley
Picture Research: Cecilia Weston-Baker
Illustrator: Ron Hayward Associates

ISBN 0-531-17204-X

Library of Congress Catalog
Card Number 89-81598

Printed in Belgium

All rights reserved

The back cover shows European Community leaders in 1989.

The author, Elizabeth Roberts, writes on current affairs, specializing in East-West relations.

EUROPE 1992
THE UNITED STATES OF EUROPE?

ELIZABETH ROBERTS

A WATTS/GLOUCESTER BOOK

Contents

Chapter One
A brief history of Europe .... p 4

This chapter gives an account of the history of Europe, which led up to the founding of the European Community.

Chapter Two
The community is born .... p 16

This outlines the setting up of the community. It explains the relations between the different countries.

Chapter Three
Deadline 1992 .... p 20

This explains what is meant by the single European market and how it will affect the rest of the world.

Factfile 1
The European Community .... p 28

Factfile 2
The EC economy .... p 30

Factfile 3
The EC administration .... p 32

Chronology .... p 34

Glossary .... p 35

Index .... p 36

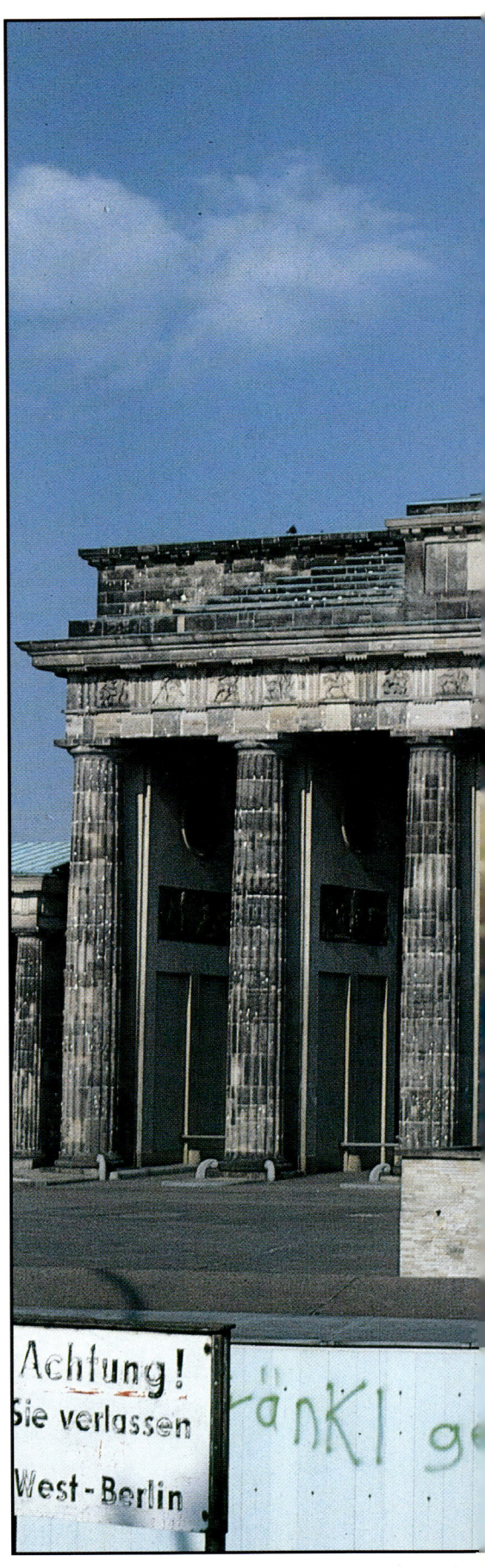

▷ The Brandenburg Gate lies between East and West Berlin in Germany. Until December 1989 it was the symbol of a divided Europe, riven by centuries of wars. The last war in Europe, World War II, in which much of Berlin was destroyed, convinced some European countries that Europe needed an organization which would eliminate disputes between nations. Out of this the European Community was born.

In 1992 12 European countries have decided to join together to form a single market. The countries of the European Community (EC), as the 12 are known, have decided to build their future together, after centuries of rivalry. The 12 member states of the European Community are: Belgium, Denmark, the Federal Republic of Germany, France, Greece, Ireland, Italy, Luxembourg, the Netherlands, Portugal, Spain and the United Kingdom. They all (except Ireland) are part of the Western bloc allied with the United States. The Eastern bloc consists of countries allied with the Soviet Union.

The EC countries, with a combined population of 320 million people (compared with the United States' 240 million, and the Soviet Union's 283 million), occupy the western edge of the great continental land mass of Eurasia, bounded by the Atlantic Ocean to the west and the Mediterranean Sea to the south. Sea trade between Europe and the other parts of the world developed early because of Europe's position, surrounded on three sides by water free of ice all year round, and on the fourth by a great continental land mass.

The climate of Europe is, on the whole, a kind one. The rainfall and average temperatures are moderate. This fact also helped Europe develop its agriculture and its industry, because communications were not blocked by desert or snow. Almost all European Community countries derive their language from one prehistoric tongue called Indo-European. Now, nearly every country has a different language: French, Spanish, Portuguese, Dutch, Danish, German, Italian, English and Greek.

The EC countries are all democracies. That is the only condition of membership, besides being European. Democracy means that they are governed by elected parliaments and more than one party contest elections.

Each member state also sends representatives to a European parliament to which a 17-person executive commission is answerable. In turn, this commission passes proposals to a council of ministers which passes laws for the community, while the commission runs many of its day to day affairs. A court of 13 independent judges settles disputes in community law, but each country retains its own system of justice for internal matters. Last but not least, the economies of all the countries in the European Community are welfare capitalist, that is to say, free enterprise and the ownership of private property is encouraged, while the state takes care of many social needs.

A brief history of Europe

The development of a sense of Europe started with the Roman Empire. It became fractured as nation states began to evolve in the 15th century. The struggle between Germany and France dominated Europe for centuries and culminated in two world wars.

△ The Parthenon in Athens is a great monument of Greek civilization. Modern architects still draw inspiration from Ancient Greek ideas.

Each of the 12 member states of the European Community has its own distinctive history and culture. But these European countries have a lot in common. Geographically, of course, they share the same sector of the globe. Culturally, too, they incorporate to a greater or lesser extent the common elements of western civilization. There is such a thing as "European-ness." If a European were dropped into another town in Europe he or she would know how to get around. Basically it's because of the layout – there is usually a church, or city hall, and streets radiating from the old center, stores and cafes where people walk and talk all day long and late into the night.

Most European countries share the artistic and intellectual heritage of Greece and Rome, Christianity, the Renaissance of learning and the development of humanism, the effects of the religious Reformation, foreign conquests and the making and losing of empires, pioneering science and technology, and the long practice of capitalism and democracy.

The heritage of Greece and Rome

The civilization which developed in Greece and Italy from around the 5th century BC gave birth to western poetry, drama, history, law, philosophy, art, science and mathematics. Greek sculpture and architecture are still regarded as models of excellence. Greek philosophical method is also still studied today by western students and scholars as an essential tool for debating questions such as the nature of truth and beauty.

Democracy, which was first practiced in Greece, is considered the fairest system of government. In a democracy, all adult citizens regularly elect members of a parliament from any number of political parties. In 5th century Greece some cities had a system known as direct democracy. The citizens would meet in the market place to discuss problems and then vote on what to do about them. However only freemen were allowed to vote – women and slaves were excluded.

The Romans extended the achievement of the Greeks by bringing the rule of law and a physically well-ordered society to much of Europe after military conquest. The Romans built great roads, bridges and aqueducts (water pipelines) and many present-day European cities are sited on Roman settlements. There are Roman remains throughout Europe – amphitheaters, temples, villas and baths.

▽ A Roman mosaic in Sicily. From central heating and interior decoration to bridges and the rule of law, the Romans left their mark on Europe.

Christianity

Christianity began to spread throughout the Roman Empire until by 300 AD (after the birth of Christ) there were Christian strongholds in France, Germany, Italy and Spain. Christianity became the official religion of the Empire in 391 and it added a vital new element to world civilization.

The message of Christianity was that since the Son of God (Jesus Christ) had come down to Earth to save mankind, everyone could be saved. This meant that every individual life was valuable in the eyes of God. Jesus Christ taught that "the meek shall inherit the Earth" and that love should govern all human actions. It was a message of hope to all people and many were converted to it. The effect of this revolutionary creed was astonishing: it changed European art and architecture by inspiring great religious paintings, frescoes and churches, as well as choral music. It also provided a new moral framework, because Christians believed in eternal life.

The Dark Ages

The Roman Empire split in two and in the 5th century AD the western part fell to invading armies from the East. (The eastern part endured until 1453.) From the 5th century onward Europe went through a period known as the Dark Ages, when learning was restricted to a few monasteries. Between the 5th and the 8th centuries there was also a gradual shift away from the old centers of classical civilization around the Mediterranean, toward the north where the valley of the Rhine is situated.

A great Christian king emerged to rule over this central (or Frankish) kingdom: his name was Charlemagne, which means Charles the Great. He was crowned Emperor in 800, and during his reign encouraged learning and spread Christianity into pagan lands. He also brought in craftsmen from Constantinople (the capital of the eastern Roman Empire and present-day Istanbul). They produced treasures and beautified his court at Aachen.

Meanwhile along the coast of western Europe and as far south and east as Sicily and Kiev (in the modern Soviet Union), pagan warriors from Scandinavia, the Vikings, were looting and pillaging. Eventually, they settled in the lands they had come to sack, and their kings (called Normans – Norsemen) became Christians ruling over the various kingdoms, including one which incorporated parts of both England and western France.

△ The Emperor Charlemagne (742-814) ruled over a Christian empire which included much of modern France and Germany.

▽ By 1500 Europe was Christian. Religion gave purpose and meaning to life, a deep wellspring for a whole civilization of arts and learning. It gave people from different countries a common experience.

CHRISTIANITY IN EUROPE

- Coptic Christians (Egypt)
- Orthodox Christians
- Catholic Christians
- Original Catholic Christians
- Celtic churches
- Islam
- Unbelievers

The Middle Ages

By 1500 AD most of Europe was Christian. The Church was not only the dominant spiritual force, but also enormously rich in lands and politically powerful. Enduring physical expressions of this might are the great Gothic cathedrals, such as Winchester in England and Chartres in France. Although this whole great Christian empire was in one sense ruled by the Pope as head of the Church, there were also kings and queens, dukes and duchesses ruling different countries. Among some of the people in these European countries there was a growing sense of national identity.

When the Normans had conquered England in 1066, they had kept their possessions in France. Joan of Arc (1412-1431) encouraged the French king to fight and expel the English from France. In Spain, Queen Isabella and King Ferdinand united Spain as a Christian nation when they conquered the last of the Islamic cities in Spain – Granada – in 1492. But the idea of a "nation," and a "nationality," in the sense of belonging to – and being willing to fight and die for – a country rather than a region or religious idea, is comparatively modern. Italy and Germany, for instance, were not unified into nation states until the middle of the 19th century, three or four hundred years after France and Spain. Yugoslavia and Czechoslovakia became nations in the 20th century.

A new society

In the Middle Ages the feudal system, where knights and peasants were bound to work for a lord in exchange for having land, came under attack. In the towns craftsmen set up their own organizations, known as guilds, so they could obtain charters of rights and practice their trade free from the interference of the church or local nobles. These free citizens developed the traditions of honesty and public service, necessary for democracy in a modern state.

▽ Fountains Abbey was built in England by 12th century Benedictine monks. The monks took part in the wool trade, making the abbey rich.

The Age of Discovery

Throughout their history, Europeans have looked outward to the rest of the world. The Portuguese explored the west coast of Africa and around the Cape of Good Hope across to India in the 15th century. A Genoese sea captain called Christopher Columbus tried to sail to India by going west across the Atlantic Ocean. In 1492 the words "the New World" were first used to describe his discovery of the islands of the Caribbean. These islands are known to this day as the West Indies because Columbus thought (mistakenly) that by sailing as far west as possible, he had arrived in India!

In Europe the first universities were founded as early as the 12th century. Universities were places where people could study subjects such as law, medicine and philosophy, as well as theology. The Renaissance is the name given to the great flowering of learning and the arts in 15th and 16th century Europe. Printing was invented in Europe (as it had been in China many centuries before) in about 1450 by Johannes Gutenburg in Mainz. The first printed book in Europe was the Gutenburg bible in 1455. Printing speeded the transmission of ideas as more books became

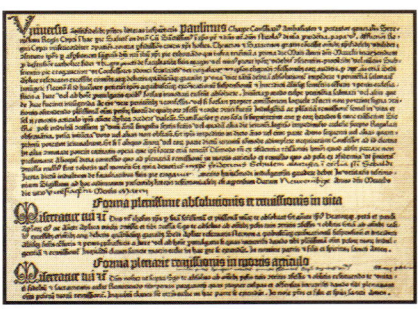

△ Printing revolutionized learning and led to social change. Illustrated above is the handwritten Irish Book of Kells (top) and a Gutenburg printed page (above).

◁ The discovery of the Americas by Christopher Columbus in 1492 led to the unprecedented spread of one civilization – the European – across the globe. This transformed the world as Europe colonized other countries to increase its wealth. Columbus' voyage had been financed by King Ferdinand and Queen Isabella of Spain.

▽ Louis XIV of France (1638-1715) provided the perfect model of the absolute ruler to other European princes. He had power over all appointments and courtiers maneuvered for royal favor. He embarked on foreign wars and took advantage of treaties with the Dutch and British to make France the most powerful country in Europe.

available. Before printing, all books had to be individually copied by hand.

The domination of the church over all learning waned as scholars eagerly rediscovered Greek and Roman texts, love poems and early adventure stories. This non-religious learning is called humanism because it is centered on human needs and values. Europeans also learned mathematics and medicine from their contact with Islamic countries where these sciences were highly developed. Learned men began to question the central role of the church.

The Reformation

Modern European history begins with the Reformation – the fragmentation of Christianity from about 1517 into two strands: Protestantism and Roman Catholicism. The Protestants broke with the Pope and set up their own, often nationally based, religions. The political consequences of this break were far-reaching. The Reformation was, at the outset, an attempt to clean up corrupt practices in the Christian church, such as the encouragement to buy eternal salvation through money rather than by living a pious life. However, the effect of questioning the authority of the Pope in Rome also led in time to the questioning of the rule of the kings, whose authority was seen as divine.

The idea arose that all citizens should not only be free to practice their religious beliefs, but also to have a say in the laws and people governing them. In England, when King Henry VIII chose to defy the Pope in 1531, he asked parliament to ratify his authority, thereby confirming parliament's central role in legitimate government.

In many other European countries, however, the weakening of papal rule led to the kings becoming absolute rulers. This meant that they were answerable to no one apart from – notionally – God. Following this upheaval the Catholic church fought back to reassert itself with the Counter-Reformation. There were religious wars in many European countries. The Thirty Years' War, one result of the conflict between Protestants and Roman Catholics, left much of central Europe in ruins and the people impoverished. The Peace of Westphalia, which ended the Thirty Years' War in 1648, marked the end of the era of religious wars in Europe. For the next 150 years France was the dominant power in Europe. King Louis XIV extended France's boundaries in the north and east, and, despite a few defeats toward the end of his reign, was able to outmaneuver his enemies.

The French Revolution
In the two hundred years between 1700 and 1900, the pace of political and economic change in various parts of Europe differed enormously. But a major landmark was the French Revolution in 1789. The absolute ruler, King Louis XVI, was violently overthrown. The slogan of the French revolution was "Liberty, equality, fraternity." Civil rights were now firmly on the European agenda. Further spasms of political unrest rocked the thrones of Europe in 1848, as the – eventually successful – pressure for change grew. Karl Marx, a German, published his ideas in *The Communist Manifesto*. This led to the spread of socialist ideas throughout 19th-century Europe.

Europe in the 19th century was the birthplace of scientists and thinkers whose work shaped the modern world – giants such as Charles Darwin in biology and

> **Citizenship**
> The concept of citizenship developed in Roman times. But the first modern expression of the idea that government gets its just powers from the consent of those who are governed is found in the first words of the US constitution in 1787 "We the People ...." The new French constitution in 1791 also set out the individual's rights in relation to the state.

△ In 1793 King Louis XVI of France was executed in the name of the people. The French Revolution occurred at a time of famine in the French countryside and complaints about high taxation in the towns. The revolution got rid of many feudal and legal inequalities, but at the cost of much bloodshed (the "Terror"). Eventually Napoleon Bonaparte became military dictator and emperor.

Albert Einstein in physics. Engineers like George Stephenson with his steam locomotive made railways possible, and Europe grew rich by providing the rest of the world with ships and engines and other kinds of technology. The industrial revolution, which had started in 18th century Britain, led to demands for raw materials. These often came from the furthest parts of the globe and were processed in the mills and workshops of Europe. This resulted in a move to grab territory abroad, which gained pace in the 19th century, making European merchants and their governments rich and powerful.

EUROPE'S COLONIAL EMPIRES IN 1914

World War I

By 1900 most of Europe west of a line drawn from Stettin in the north to Trieste on the borders of Italy was organized into nation states, vying with each other in shifting alliances for domination. War was still considered the necessary last resort to solve international disputes or gain territorial advantage. France had fought – and been defeated by – a newly-unified Germany in 1870/71.

Then, in 1914, an apparently insignificant event in a remote part of eastern Europe plunged Europe into a great war. The assassination of Austrian Archduke Franz Ferdinand in June 1914 tripped a series of complex military alliances; and within a month all of Europe had mobilized. Austria-Hungary declared war on Serbia in eastern Europe, which was allied to Russia. Germany, in alliance with Austria-Hungary, declared war on Russia. Britain and France joined Russia in a war that was supposed to last a few months, but went on for four long years. The casualty figures were horrifying. About nine million soldiers, sailors and airmen died. The armies fought a more or less static campaign, firing at each other from trenches.

Russia was knocked out of the war in 1917 when there was a revolution, in which the Tzar and his family were deposed and then murdered. A communist government inspired by Karl Marx's ideas swept the old order away. The German kaiser was also forced to abdicate as the German army ran out of supplies and morale. Germany signed an armistice in 1918.

- British
- French
- German
- Portuguese
- Spanish
- Dutch
- Belgian
- Italian
- Ottoman (Turkish)
- Danish
- Rest of the world

△ By 1914 four-fifths of the world was under the rule of a European country. The drive for foreign conquests was not solely inspired by the greed for wealth; many Europeans thought that they would bring the benefits of their (superior they believed) civilization to their colonies. The Europeans also exploited their colonies for their natural resources and manpower, which caused much pain and bitterness. In many former colonies these feelings are still strong.

World War II

The peace treaty signed at Versailles in 1919 after World War I imposed heavy penalties on the Germans. This led to social and economic difficulties, and in turn to the rise of the Nazi leader, Adolf Hitler. He dragged Germany into another war. This became a global war when Japan attacked the US naval base at Pearl Harbor in December 1941. By the end of World War II, the European age – the age during which Europe had dominated the world – seemed to be over.

During World War II (1939-45), more than 40 million people were killed in Europe alone. The economic devastation was as great as the loss of human life. Factories and towns were destroyed, food was rationed and there was no work. In Germany in 1946, anything could be bought for a package of cigarettes – paper money was worthless. In post-war France and Italy, governments came and went, split between squabbling factions of the right and the left. Britain, once the proud possessor of a world empire, was in colossal debt to the United States for war supplies.

△ Adolf Hitler (1889-1945) preached a dangerous mixture of racial hatred and extreme nationalism. He led Germany into World War II, which resulted in its division.

▽ By the end of World War II many German cities, such as Bremen (below), were reduced to rubble by Allied aerial bombing.

Post-war Europe

During World War II the Soviet armies occupied vast areas of eastern Europe including East Germany. Once the war was over, they stayed in place. Europe was now divided into democracies in the west and communist-dominated countries in the east. An "iron curtain" had fallen across Europe. Later it became known that the ruler of the Soviet Union, Josef Stalin, had caused the death of millions of Soviet citizens during his reign of terror in the 1930s and after.

Was there any way to prevent further bloodshed in Europe? This issue became even more pressing after the invention of the atomic bomb, which the United States had invented in 1945 and which the Soviet Union acquired in 1949. One man certainly thought so. Jean Monnet's idea of a European community was to bring lasting peace and prosperity to Europe through economic and political cooperation and shared institutions. He liked to quote the Swiss philosopher Henri-Frédéric Amiel: "Each man's experience starts again from the beginning. Only institutions grow wiser; they accumulate collective experience, and owing to this experience and this wisdom, men subject to the same rules will not see their own nature changing, but their behavior gradually transformed."

△ Above: Josef Stalin (1879-1953) was in command of the Soviet armed forces during World War II. It took four years for the Allied armies to defeat the Germans. Top: Soviet troops hand out food to Polish people in 1945. The Soviet armies remained in eastern Europe after the war and forced those countries to accept communist governments.

Jean Monnet (1888-1979) was born in Cognac, the traditional center of brandy-making in France. When he was a young man, Monnet traveled in the United States and Canada selling brandy. He lived in London for a while, where he learned English. He also learned the traditions of the City of London, where a man's word is as good as his bond, that is, any verbal agreement was binding. When World War I broke out in 1914 he was 26, but he was debarred from military service on health grounds. However, he observed that the French and the British who were fighting on the same side in the war against the Germans, were duplicating much of their war effort, particularly in the use of shipping and supplies. He persuaded the authorities to appoint him coordinator of an Allied Supply Committee.

His success in this job led to his appointment, at the age of 31, as Deputy Secretary-General of the League of Nations, the organization set up after the war with the goal of settling international disputes without fighting. Unfortunately, the member states were not willing to sacrifice their national interests in favor of the common good. France won heavy economic damages and territory from Germany after World War I, which led to both bitterness and political unrest in Germany, and ultimately to World War II.

Jean Monnet left the League of Nations in 1923 to take over his family brandy business in Cognac. In 1926 he left France again, this time to set up an international commercial bank in the United States. His travels took him to Poland, Sweden and China. He advised the Polish government in Warsaw during a currency crisis. In China he met the nationalist leader, Chiang Kaishek and advised him on modernizing the railways. In 1936, Monnet returned to political action, realizing that another war in Europe was possible. The French Prime Minister Edouard Daladier sent him on a secret mission to the United States in 1938 to buy military aircraft. His negotiations were successful, despite the fact that at the time the United States was bound by the Neutrality Act which prohibited the export of arms to nations at war. During the early years of World War II, several hundred American warplanes and warships were delivered to help France's ally Britain.

Throughout World War II, Jean Monnet was at the center of the Allied war effort. He drafted a revolutionary Franco-British Declaration in 1940, which would have given both nations single sovereignty in the face of the impending fall of France to German troops.

▽ Jean Monnet, the father of the European Community, (in the center of the photograph) in Luxembourg in 1952, when the European Coal and Steel Community (ECSC) was formed under his leadership. This was a practical achievement, of enormous importance because it was a revolutionary approach to international relations. The countries that joined the ECSC were giving up their sovereignty in two crucial industries to an independent authority. France had not signed a treaty with Germany at the end of World War II and the ECSC indicated both countries' willingness to work together peacefully in the future.

Although the declaration was nullified the following day by the new French Prime Minister, Marshal Henri Philippe Pétain, who had decided to collaborate with the invader, it was a landmark in international cooperation.

After the war, Monnet was made Planning Commissioner for the French economy. However, he saw that it was necessary to include Germany in the economic recovery of Europe, and in 1950 came up with the idea of the European Coal and Steel Community. This venture was a practical, achievable step toward wider economic and political cooperation, which Monnet believed was the only way to ensure peace and prosperity. Monnet remained at the center of the European movement for the rest of his life, principally in the role of leader of the Action Committee for the United States of Europe. The action committee was an influential pressure group in support of the European ideal and allowed Monnet to spread his ideas. In 1976 he was made an "Honorary Citizen of Europe" and he died in 1979 at his home at Houjarray, outside Paris.

The future unity of Europe

Jean Monnet spoke of a "ferment of change" which he saw would be created by the European Community. Monnet had faith in the ability of Europeans to adapt and cooperate in the face of challenges. He believed any European country with a democratic system of government and which shared the desire for European union should be allowed to join the community. His motto was "Set yourself a goal and move forward by stages."

The community is born

After World War II France and Germany led the focus of efforts to build for a peaceful future.

△ The Berlin Wall was built in 1961 by the communist government of East Germany to stop the flow of refugees to the West. Anyone attempting to cross the German border at any point between east and west was shot. The Wall became the most powerful symbol of the Cold War led by the two superpowers, the Soviet Union and the United States, after World War II. Europe became an armed camp with massive armies stationed in both parts of Germany.

The bitter aftermath of World War I taught European statesmen that a practical effort should be made to incorporate Germany into the post-World War II reconstruction of Europe. Also, it was clear as soon as World War II ended that the Soviet army would not be demobilized as most of the other Allied armies had been. After the end of World War II the Soviet Union had control over many countries of eastern Europe, such as Poland, Hungary and East Germany (called, misleadingly, the German Democratic Republic), and it imposed communist governments on them.

In September 1946, Britain's wartime prime minister, Winston Churchill, made a speech in Zürich calling for the establishment of a United States of Europe. The first tentative step toward such a state was made by the French foreign minister, Robert Schuman, in 1950. He took up the idea, proposed by Jean Monnet, of a European Coal and Steel Community (ECSC). In the ECSC, national governments in western Europe were asked for the first time to delegate part of their sovereignty to a High Authority. The officials of this authority were appointed by them, but once appointed, had to act independently. The first members of the ECSC were France, the Federal Republic of Germany (West Germany), Italy, Belgium, the Netherlands and the Grand Duchy of Luxembourg.

The Six

The Treaty of Paris setting up the ECSC was signed in 1951. The United Kingdom did not join the "six" because it was thought that the rules were too binding, and Britain still had close trading and other links with its overseas empire, now called the British Commonwealth.

In the excitement which followed the setting up of the ECSC, politicians drew up proposals for European power-sharing in the fields of foreign affairs, defense, economic and social integration and the protection of human rights. However, hopes were dashed when the French government vetoed plans for a European army in August 1954. Instead, the Atlantic Alliance and its military organization, the North Atlantic Treaty Organization (NATO), which included the United States, was left with the main responsibility for defending western Europe against the Soviet Union and its satellites in eastern Europe. They had signed a treaty known as the Warsaw Pact, to coordinate their defense measures. Although France was a member of the Atlantic Alliance, it had refused to join NATO.

The Treaties of Rome

The foreign ministers of the six met in Messina in Southern Italy in 1955, and decided to move ahead with more limited plans for European economic integration. After long debate, the Treaties of Rome was signed in 1957, establishing the European Economic Community (the EEC) and the European Atomic Energy Committee (Euratom).

▷ The Treaties of Rome, signed in 1957, set up the European Economic Community (EEC) and the European Atomic Energy Committee (Euratom). Four institutions administered these new bodies: the European Parliament, the Council, the Commission and the Court of Justice. Until 1967, the ECSC, Euratom and the EEC were all administered separately. Since then there has been a single commission and a single council.

The Treaties of Rome went further than providing for the free movement of goods between the founding six member states. They also provided for a number of common policies on matters such as agriculture, transportation and foreign trade, and the harmonization of laws on social policy and competition.

Seeing the success of the first efforts of the six, other countries became interested in joining the community. Greece and Turkey were granted associate status as early as 1959. But a major step was the application of Ireland, Denmark and the United Kingdom to join as full members in 1961.

While their applications were still being considered, the terms of the first European Common Agricultural Policy were agreed to in 1962 between the founding six member states. It was decided that farmers should be guaranteed prices for various farm goods like grain and animal products. Many European farmers were small landholders, who had other, part-time, jobs. Making sure farmers had a steady income was considered essential for political reasons.

△ President Charles de Gaulle of France said "non" in 1963 to Britain's application to join the EEC. He claimed that Britain only wanted to join for economic reasons and did not support the EEC's political aims.

De Gaulle says no

In 1963 European unity suffered a setback. France's leader General Charles de Gaulle blocked Britain's application to join the community, on the grounds that he doubted Britain's commitment to Europe. Weeks later, France and Germany signed a cooperation treaty. This gesture, following so soon after France's objection to Britain's membership, dealt a severe blow not only to Britain's hopes but also, for a time, to the community itself.

△ In 1967 de Gaulle and his prime minister, Georges Pompidou, met the British prime minister, Harold Wilson, and foreign minister, George Brown. Britain had to improve its relations with other European countries before being invited to join the EEC in 1972.

The 1970s
In 1974 there was an energy crisis followed by a decline in trade, which hit the European Community hard. The crisis was caused by the oil-producing countries of the Middle East raising their prices. Since 63 percent of member countries' energy requirements – mainly petroleum – came from the Middle East, countries such as France restored trade barriers to protect their economy. Also, the British government decided to renegotiate the terms of Britain's entry into the community.

During the years which followed, many tense battles were fought within the community to obtain the necessary agreement between member states to allow the EEC to grow and expand. One of the most crucial issues was whether or not the community should raise its own taxes to finance its own administration. There was also a serious crisis in 1965 when General de Gaulle objected to plans to expand the community's powers and to increase majority voting in the council.

After seven months, a compromise was reached and it was agreed that whenever a member felt that its "vital interests" were at stake, the council would try to agree on a unanimous solution. However, there was no magic formula in the case of the council's failure to do so. The United Kingdom applied to join again in 1967, and again its application was vetoed by General de Gaulle. Despite the general's objections, the community gained financial autonomy – that is, the right to raise taxes and decide how to spend money – in 1970, to be supervised by a strengthened European parliament. This met the basic democratic requirement of "no taxation without representation" and also took the community a small way toward political union.

Enlarging the community
De Gaulle resigned in 1969 and eventually, in 1972, three new members joined the community: Denmark, Ireland and the United Kingdom. In 1979 direct elections were held to the European Parliament. Until then the European Parliament had been appointed by member parliaments. Henceforth, Members of the European Parliament (known as MEPs) were to be elected by voters every five years. One of the qualifying aspects for membership of the community is that a country must be a democracy. Now the community itself was to be run more democratically. Also in 1979, the European Monetary System (EMS) was set up. The EMS has four main components: a European currency unit called the ecu, an exchange-rate and information mechanism, credit facilities and transfer arrangements. A common European currency and bank have been proposed as necessary to complete the effectiveness of the community in world trade. However, it has been difficult to persuade all member states to agree, and the United Kingdom is not fully part of it. In 1981, Greece joined the community, followed in 1986 by Spain and Portugal, making 12 member states in total.

△ Spanish Prime Minister Felipe Gonzales finally signed the treaty for Spain's entry into the European Community in Madrid on June 12, 1985. Portugal joined on the same day, making the community 12. They officially became members in 1986.

Deadline 1992

In 1986, the 12 member states of the European Community (EC) signed the Single European Act binding them to create a truly unified market within the EC by 1992. Events in 1989 in eastern Europe gave the 12 a sense of urgency about achieving greater political cohesion.

△ The European Commission in session. It proposes new laws to the European Council of Ministers. Under the Single European Act, a new cooperation procedure has been introduced giving the European Parliament a say on commission proposals.

The Single European Act, signed in 1986, commits the 12 to establish an area without internal frontiers by 1992. This means there is to be completely free movement of "goods, persons, services and capital" within the community. This apparently simple goal involves over 600 individual measures to harmonize European standards in fields as diverse as trading practices, manufacturing standards, educational qualifications and broadcasting.

The purely material potential gains for all Europeans of belonging to one community have been predicted as follows: the removal of direct frontier and other customs costs due to, for example, the waiting time for trucks and trains at the present frontiers: 9 billion ecus; savings in industrial costs because of the abolition of conflicting technical standards: 40 billion ecus; intensified competition for public purchasing – such items as street lighting, roads and school equipment: 40 billion ecus; the rationalization of industry, whereby firms join up together to enlarge their

▷ A car assembly line in Milan. European production facilities such as this ultramodern robot line making luxury Alfa Romeo cars will save billions of ecus with the creation of the 1992 Single Market.

product lines and make their sales forces more effective: 60 billion ecus; the intensification of competition generally, encouraging the growth of new small businesses: 140 billion ecus. At the present time the ecu is worth about one dollar.

European procedures

Under the Single European Act a new cooperation procedure has been introduced giving an additional say to parliament. Parliament can now give an opinion both on commission proposals and – for the first time – on the common position of the Council of Ministers. The European Parliament also has a series of specialist committees, divided by subject area. These committees examine commission proposals on agriculture, the community budget, foreign affairs, industry and so on before they are presented to parliament as a whole.

The last word on community law rests with the council. In the council an increasing number of issues can be dealt with by a "qualified majority vote." In this type of case, Germany, France, Italy and the United Kingdom have ten votes each, Spain has eight; Belgium, Greece, the Netherlands and Portugal five each, Denmark and Ireland three each and Luxembourg two. Other issues can be dealt with by simple majority voting – that is, seven of the 12 members in favor.

The German question

The original purpose of the community was to cement together, in "ever closer union," the western European democracies through shared wealth and shared institutions. Today the 12 are facing a period of rapid and unexpected change in eastern Europe. The so-called "German question" – arising from the post-World War II partition of Germany – was on the back burner, so to speak. The revival of German hopes of reunification came in 1989 with the liberalization of Soviet policy toward eastern Europe, under a reforming general secretary of the Communist Party of the Soviet Union, Mikhail Gorbachev.

In the summer of 1989 a great wave of emigration – mostly of young workers with their families – from East Germany into West Germany took place, much to the annoyance of East Germany's "conservative" Communist Party leader, Erich Honecker. After an embarrassing celebration of 40 years' communist rule, massive public demonstrations demanding greater freedom forced Honecker's resignation in October 1989. In December his successor, Egon Krenz, and the entire Communist Party leadership resigned after they had been discredited over charges of corruption. Honecker was put under house arrest and free elections are expected in 1990.

These events gave rise to traditional fears of the economic power of a reunified Germany. France – historically Germany's rival for influence on the continent of Europe – was particularly concerned. French President François Mitterand urged the community to speed up political unification.

△ Soviet President Mikhail Gorbachev came to power in 1985. Faced with economic collapse, he soon set about reforming the Soviet economy and political system.

▽ Thousands of young East Germans showed their dissatisfaction with communism by voting with their feet and leaving their country. The East German government had to lift travel restrictions.

Eastern Europe

In October 1989 Hungary declared itself to be no longer a "socialist republic," but simply a democratic republic in which parties could contest free elections, and the Communist Party – forcibly maintained in power by Soviet tanks – was to lose its "leading role."

Also in 1989 in Poland, the reforming Catholic workers' party, *Solidarnosc* (Solidarity), under the leadership of Lech Walesa, succeeded in wresting a power-sharing deal following an overwhelming victory in the elections over the ruling Communist Party, and the promise of totally free elections is on the horizon.

Even more astonishing changes occurred in Czechoslovakia, where, over a period of ten days in November 1989, massive demonstrations and strikes led to the resignation of the hard-line communist government and later on the election of a non-communist president, the playwright Vaclav Havel. Tired of living in a corrupt one-party police state, the Czechs demanded the right to elect a government from among several parties, free speech and a market economy in which businesses and services would respond to consumer demand. Finally in December 1989, after ten days of bitter fighting when thousands died, the people of Romania freed themselves of the communist tyranny of Nicolae Ceausescu and his wife Elena.

The leaders of the European Community met in a hurried session to discuss what their response should be to these unexpected and sudden changes. They agreed to a massive package of economic aid both to the Soviet Union and eastern Europe.

△ Lech Walesa is the leader of the Polish reforming Catholic workers' party, called *Solidarnosc*. It defeated the communists in elections in 1989.

▽ By 1989 food queues in the Soviet Union were worse than ever before. As well as economic problems, the Soviet Union faces internal pressures, such as ethnic violence between Armenians and Azerbaijanis.

Events in East Germany and eastern Europe have led committed Europeans to urge the European Community to develop more powerful structures which could not be unbalanced by a larger German member state or a number of eastern European associates. The argument for a single European market is not merely an economic one. The original goals of the European Community were: firstly, to end war between its members; secondly, to end economic conflict between members; thirdly, to harness their combined economic and political strength to enable them to equal the United States and the Soviet Union; and finally, to establish a new form of relations between states. The hope was to provide peace and political stability in a part of the world where nationalist arguments had led to disastrous wars and human suffering.

Relations with the rest of Europe
Neutral European countries such as Sweden, Switzerland and Austria were also reexamining their position in the light of the new developments. A report commissioned in 1989 by the Federal government in Switzerland, for example, recommended joining the European Community, because the arguments in favor of neutrality no longer applied. Switzerland's centuries-old experience of multilingual federation between largely self-governing small "cantons" would be a valuable contribution to a new Europe "without frontiers." Since the European market of the 12 is nearly half the world market, the internal improvements promised by 1992 should benefit the world.

◁ An aerial view of the French end of the tunnel being built to link Britain and France in 1993. If trade between European countries is to grow, then the community needs rapid, barrier-free transport. The tunnel will speed up the journey from the rest of Europe to Britain and cut down Britain's feeling of being separate from the continent. Critics of Britain's attitude to Europe point out that Britain has been extremely slow about deciding on where to route a rail link from the tunnel to London.

△ Bananas from the Windward Islands in the Caribbean are unloaded in Wales. The European Community guarantees the prices of such exports and this provides stability for the planners and people of the Third World.

Outside Europe

The community has had ties with countries outside Europe since 1963, when Turkey was welcomed as an associate member, and the first Yaoundé Convention was signed between the community and 17 African countries.

Later, the Lomé Convention (1975) provided for commercial cooperation between the community and 46 countries of Africa, the Caribbean and the Pacific (ACP). In 1979 a second Lomé Convention was signed with 66 ACP countries. Virtually all products originating from the ACP countries have free access to the community market, and the convention guarantees those countries stable export earnings from 36 basic commodities such as coffee and sugar. Third World countries are thus shielded from the ups and downs of the prices fetched by their produce on world markets. The Lomé Convention also provides for industrial cooperation between the community and the ACP countries through joint institutions in which both parties have their say on the way things are done.

In 1975, the community signed a similar agreement with Israel. In 1976, the community also made an agreement with the countries of the Maghreb (Tunisia, Algeria and Morocco) and of the Mashrea (Egypt, Syria, Jordan and Lebanon).

The European Community is aware of the needs of the Third World, to which it owes much of the prosperity of the last 200 years. Cheap raw materials and agricultural products helped Europe industrialize in the 19th and 20th centuries. Aid from Europe to the developing countries is aimed primarily at enabling them to take on responsibility for their own development. The average income of a person in the Third World is 920 ecus compared with 9,300 ecus of someone in Western Europe – ten times less.

Aid from the community runs at about 0.3 percent of the Gross National Product (GNP or total income) of the community, or some 36,000 million ecus. Third World countries are crippled by debt, amounting to almost half their annual GNP. Despite the EC contribution, which has risen in real terms every year since 1975, aid is only managing to keep up with the needs of the poor in Africa and Asia, since a growing population makes ever increasing demands on resources. Occasionally there are acute crises, such as the famines in Ethiopia. In cases such as these, when four million people were suddenly known to be at risk, the European Community made an instant contribution of money and materials.

Europe and the United States

Since the end of World War II, the United States has taken great responsibility for the security and prosperity of Western Europe. Now, thanks to the momentous changes in Eastern Europe, it looks as if that responsibility will diminish and change.

At the end of the war in 1945, the United States provided economic aid to a battered and broke western Europe through the Marshall Plan. Later, by joining with 15 other countries in the North Atlantic Treaty Organization (NATO), the United States provided massive military resources in western Europe to contain the threat of communist expansion.

For the time being, and according to the Treaties of Rome, national security is not a matter for the European Community. Western leaders have agreed that the instability caused by the great melting of the icepack in eastern Europe makes the existence of NATO, backed by the United States, more necessary than ever. However, both superpowers are engaged in negotiations to reduce the number of troops stationed in Europe, which would have far-reaching economic effects.

Although the United States welcomes the rapid development of the European single market, there are occasional hiccups. For example, the United States objects when European standards in meat or fruit appear to exclude American products or penalize them unfairly.

△ President George Bush of the United States (center) at talks with the Soviet president, Mikhail Gorbachev (right), in Malta, December 1989. At this summit Gorbachev proposed an international conference to discuss the future of Europe.

The future

There are many social, political and economic issues facing the community in the future. One problem is that of attempted immigration into Europe. Britain faces urgent demands from millions of citizens of its Far Eastern colony of Hong Kong to give them rights to British citizenship – and, by extension, to the European Community. Hong Kong people are worried about communist repressions when the People's Republic of China repossesses the territory in the year 1997.

Already some people in West Germany and France resent the workers who have come from Turkey and Morocco, in search of work and a better standard of living. A flood of "economic refugees" from eastern European countries, such as Yugoslavia and Poland, could also present a further challenge to the comparatively young institutions of the community.

The community also faces the problem of protecting the environment. Centuries of industrial expansion and urban growth have polluted Europe's rivers and destroyed the countryside. The Alps, one of the world's great wildernesses, is under threat because too many tourists want to spend time there.

Another issue which will not go away is the nagging one of national sovereignty: should there just be cooperation between European countries or should there be a federation, where the countries are more tightly bound together. A "United States of Europe" was indeed in the minds of the original signatories of the Treaties of Rome. However, the British government is one of those countries which is reluctant to give control over its currency and budget to Europe.

The events of 1989 in eastern Europe have altered the political and economic map beyond the EC boundaries. The hope of democratic government and freer trade in this wider arena increase the chances of peace and prosperity for all the citizens of Europe.

▽ In 1989 Hong Kong protesters took to the streets. They were worried about what would happen to the 5.7 million inhabitants of Britain's Far Eastern colony when it is handed over to communist China in 1997. Hong Kong people want British citizenship, which would give them the freedom to live and work anywhere in Europe after 1992.

▷ Jacques Delors is the president of the European Commission. In 1989 he caused a stir by urging members of the EC to move more rapidly toward monetary union. He also wants greater progress toward political union.

The European Community

The European Community is made up of 12 independent states, each with its own government. It has 320 million people speaking nine different official languages. Despite their cultural and historical differences, they have all voted to join together to live in peace. They want to work together to improve their standard of living and give Europe a bigger say in world affairs than if they remained separate. The peoples of Europe have fought each other for centuries, but now they are determined to settle differences by peaceful negotiation and to strive for more justice and prosperity.

Belgium is a small, flat, prosperous country with a short (40 mi) coastline stretching along the North Sea. Almost 47 percent of its land surface is used for agriculture and 20 percent is forest. Coal is mined in two large centers. The capital city is Brussels, headquarters of the European Commission. Belgium is a parliamentary democracy with a hereditary monarchy. Legislative power is shared by the king, the Chamber of Representatives and the Senate. The official languages are Flemish and French. German is spoken by a minority in the East. The population is 9.9 million.

Denmark has an area of 16,633 sq miles. Although 66 percent of the land is used for agriculture, it has increasingly valuable oil and natural gas deposits in the North Sea. The capital is Copenhagen. The national language is Danish, although a minority in the south speak German. Almost all Danes belong to the established Evangelical-Lutheran Church. Major exports are foodstuffs, furniture and clothing, machinery and chemicals. Denmark produces food for 5 million people. Denmark is a constitutional monarchy and a parliamentary democracy.

Federal Republic of Germany (West Germany) covers an area of 95,975 sq miles bounded to the north by the North Sea and the Baltic and to the south by the Alps. The Federal Republic is only part of Germany. The "other Germany" is called the German Democratic Republic, and is not a member of the European Community. The FRG is the richest country in the community. Its capital is Bonn and it has a population of 61 million, more or less equally divided between Protestants and Catholics. It is a democratic parliamentary state with a federal constitution. It has a president as head of state and a chancellor who is the head of the federal government. A small minority in the north speak Danish.

France with an area of 220,668 sq miles is the largest country in the community, with a population of 55.6 million whose official language is French. Some 58 percent of the land is used for agriculture. Almost all French citizens are Roman Catholics. France is a republic in which power is shared between the president, the government and the parliament. The capital is Paris.

Greece has 2,000 islands in a total land area of 51,146 sq miles. Some 75 percent of the land is used for agriculture, which, together with tourism and shipping make up its principal industries. Greece has 9.9 million inhabitants, most of whom belong to the Greek Orthodox church. Greece is a parliamentary democracy with a president and prime minister.

Ireland lies to the furthest northwest of the community and has a land area of 27,137 sq miles. It is a very rural country. Some 95 percent of the population of 3.5 million are Roman Catholic. Ireland is a parliamentary democracy with a president and a prime minister. The capital is Dublin.

Italy has an area of 116,303 sq miles. The capital is Rome and the national language of the population of 57.1 million is Italian. Most Italians are Roman Catholics. Italy is a parliamentary republic. The president is elected by parliament and he appoints a prime minister.

Luxembourg is a small country – only 998 sq miles. The capital city is also called Luxembourg, and is home to the European Community's Court of Justice. The population is 366,000 with a high proportion of foreigners (26 percent). "Letzeburgesch" is the national language. Luxembourg is a center for banking and international business. Some 95 percent of the population are Roman Catholics, and they are ruled by a grand duke and a chamber of deputies.

The Netherlands has an area of 15,770 sq miles, lying very low. The biggest city is Amsterdam although the seat of government is at The Hague. With a population of 14.5 million, it is the most densely populated country in the world at 931 inhabitants per sq mi. The Netherlands is a parliamentary democracy with a queen.

Portugal has a long – 518 mi – Atlantic coastline and a total land area of 36,390 sq miles. The capital is Lisbon and the national language of the 10.2 million inhabitants is Portuguese. Most Portuguese are Roman Catholics. Although the land is heavily wooded (48 percent), nearly all the rest of the land is used for agriculture. Portugal exports textiles as well as machinery, pulp and paper, wood and cork and foodstuffs. It is a parliamentary republic.

Spain has an area of 194,896 sq miles. There are 39.6 million inhabitants and the official language is Spanish. The predominant religion is Roman Catholicism and its capital is Madrid. Tourism is very important for Spain's economy. Spain is a constitutional monarchy with a parliament. The king is head of state and commander-in-chief of the armed forces.

United Kingdom has an area of 94,226 sq miles, mainly consisting of England, Scotland and Wales. A fourth part of the country, Ulster, is in Northern Ireland. Some 77 percent of the land is used for agriculture and coal and iron ore are mined. The capital is London and the population 56.6 million. Most British people belong to the Anglican or Protestant churches, but in Northern Ireland about 35 percent of the population is Roman Catholic. Britain is a parliamentary democracy with a queen. The UK has high technology industries and services, including financial ones centered in the City of London.

The EC economy

The economy of Europe, although devastated by World War II, is now one of the strongest in the world. Europe has been industrialized for two centuries. In the last 25 years Europeans have doubled their income, having twice as many goods and services at their disposal as they had in 1965. This compares with an increase of only 60 percent in the United States and an increase of 400 percent in Japan. However, US income is higher than European income.

Wealth
Community income is measured in ECUs – European Currency Units, based on the average exchange rate for various European currencies on the world markets. The ecu is currently worth about one dollar.

The total combined Gross Domestic Product (GDP) of the European 12 was 3,314 million ecus in 1985 compared with Japan's 1,754 million and the United States's massive 5,172 million.

Within the community there are great differences both within and between countries. The regions of Extremadura within Spain and Limousin within France are comparatively poor. Luxembourg, Denmark and the Federal Republic of Germany (FRG) as a whole are rich compared with Spain, Greece and Portugal.

Agriculture
Europe's success compared with some other parts of the world is shown by the regular surpluses of food produced. Until recently, Europe had embarrassing butter and meat "mountains" (surpluses kept very expensively in store) as well as wine and oil "lakes."

These surpluses were caused by a political decision to encourage stable prices by guaranteeing small farmers a return on their produce. A number of Europeans, especially in southern Germany, are part-time farmers, cultivating a small plot of land in the evenings and on weekends, as well as working in local industry.

This system has produced prosperous rural communities in marked contrast to the poverty and inefficiency of the centralized and collectivized agricultures of eastern Europe, where small farmers were forced to give up their land and work under a bureaucratic system for large cooperatives.

Productivity varies within the community according to the type of cultivation: 30 people per acre work the land in crop-intensive areas such as Italy and Spain, whereas only 10 per acre are needed for livestock (beef and milk cattle or pigs) in Northern Europe.

Energy
The community produces more than half the energy it consumes, but that still means that it is heavily dependent on importing such commodities as oil and gas. There are five sources of primary energy: oil, coal, natural gas, nuclear energy and hydroelectricity. Oil is the community's main source of energy supply (45 percent) and nuclear energy is very important in France, where it provides 70 percent of energy.

ENERGY RESOURCES
- Oilfields
- Natural gas fields
- Coalfields
- Major nuclear and hydroelectric stations

MINERAL RESOURCES
- Gold
- Silver
- Lead
- Zinc
- Tin
- Iron Ore
- Nickel
- Bauxite
- Copper
- Uranium

Industry

Europe depends, to a large extent, on the Third World for its raw materials. It imports nearly all its copper, iron ore, nickel and phosphates. Once a major world producer of iron and steel, ships and cars, Europe now has booming service industries. Transportation, banking, and tourism are some examples of services. This move from heavy and manufacturing industries to services is sometimes called "post-industrial" economy. For a while, the transition process had a drastic effect on European levels of employment, since more than 4 million jobs were lost from old industries.

Europe and the Third World

Some 3,700 million people live in the Third World. Their average annual income is only 920 ecus a year, compared with European 9,300 ecus. Europe feels a responsibility to help Third World countries develop their economies. Europeans developed trade with many territories during the period of European colonial expansion. Having regained their independence, these countries continue to supply raw materials to Europe. Aid is sent from Europe to enable the poorer countries of the world to industrialize and develop in an attempt to correct the imbalance in this relationship.

Other external trade

The European Community is the leading trading power in the world, accounting for nearly 20 percent of world trade. By 1986, more than half the EC's total imports were of manufactured goods. The community's main suppliers are the United States and the EFTA countries comprising Norway, Sweden, Finland, Austria and Switzerland. The community has a balance of trade surplus with the rest of the world.

▽ A French farmer ploughs his fields the traditional way before planting some new vines.

The EC administration

Like the United Nations and the British Commonwealth, the European Community is an effort to build a just, peaceful and prosperous world. However the European Community is unique because, while each member state so far has kept its independence and autonomy, common institutions have been created where proposals can be discussed and decisions made for the benefit of all.

The Council of Ministers
The Council of 12 ministers, one from each member state, is the decision-making body of the community. The council is chaired in turn by each member state for six months. For instance, for the first half of 1990 the chair is held by Ireland, in the second half by Italy, then the Netherlands.

The European Commission
The Commission proposes community legislation to the council. There are 17 members of the Commission, each appointed for four years. They are not there to represent their own country's interests, but those of the community as a whole. The president of the European Commission is Jacques Delors, who will see Europe through to 1992.

The European Parliament
The European Parliament has grown in importance since 1979, when members were first elected by direct universal adult suffrage. The 518 members are elected for five years and they group together on the basis of political tendency rather than nationality. Parliament's job is to watch over the budget and the operation of the work of the commission. It intervenes in the law-making process and can sack the commission.

The new cooperation procedure 1986
Under the new procedure the Council of Ministers does not have the final say on any new EC law. Parliament has the right to amend or reject the council's position on a new law if a majority of its members agree to this. The council may then adopt a new law if there is a majority for it.

The European Commission
It proposes any new laws and then takes parliament's opinion before submitting it to the council.

▽ The European Community headquarters in Brussels. It houses all the committees and administration of the EC. The European Parliament sits in Strasbourg in France.

The Court of Justice interprets all EC laws and acts independently. Anyone can bring a case against his or her government to this court.

The European Parliament watches over the working of the Commission and discusses new laws. Elections to it are held every five years.

The Council of Ministers is composed of ministers from the 12 member states. It is the decision-making body of the EC.

The Court of Justice

The Court of Justice of the European Communities is based in Luxembourg. Its task is to interpret the European Constitution and the application of community laws. It has 13 judges, one from each country plus one to make an odd number. Judgments of the court are binding on each member country, and its independence is guaranteed.

Other EC bodies

Other European Community bodies include: the Economic and Social Committee, based in Brussels; the Commission is bound to consult its 189 members, who represent employers, trade unions and consumers, on proposals relating to economic and social matters; the Court of Auditors who monitor the spending of European revenues; and the European Investment Bank, which lends money for capital projects to help the community grow.

The Common Agricultural Policy (CAP)

was begun in 1962. It provides subsidies for community food. At one time it created butter "mountains" and wine "lakes" far in excess of community needs. For the last four years, food surpluses have dwindled, and support prices to the farmer have dropped by 10 percent. In February 1989 the Council of Ministers fixed the annual amount by which CAP spending could rise in real terms until 1992 – 1.9 percent instead of the 7.5 percent average in previous years. However, support for farmers is a sensitive political and social issue in the community which has 10 million farmers compared with only 3.8 million in the United States and five million in Japan.

The European Agricultural Guidance and Guarantee Fund

looks after Europe's forests. In fact Europe has only four percent of the world's forest resources and 172 million ecus is being spent on projects to improve timber stocks.

The Common Fisheries Policy

protects stocks of fish within community waters and deals with the interests of the fishing industry.

The European Space Agency

trains between 40 and 50 graduates a year in its Horizon 2000 program in the Netherlands.

The Social Fund

gives financial help to training and employment schemes, particularly in areas of high unemployment, for young people and for the disabled.

The Regional Development Fund

was set up in 1975 to help parts of the EC situated in difficult geographical areas or areas of high unemployment. Further guarantees of job security, minimum wages and worker participation in the running of industry are envisaged in the "Social Charter," proposed for discussion by the president of the European Commission, Jacques Delors. Work is also in progress on the harmonization of standards – from medical qualifications to light bulbs, in order to make EC living a reality. Broadcasting is to be regulated within the EC by a convention which will set viewing standards, limiting violence and pornography, and encourage European program makers. New technology such as satellite broadcasting will make international broadcasting easier and there will be common technical standards for European hardware to receive programs.

Chronology

The early Roman Empire brought the rule of law to Europe, but it was swept aside by barbarian armies from the east. The Dark Ages gave way to a period of great progress where wars were part of the growth of nation states. In the 19th century most European countries enjoyed a long period of peace. This was shattered by two world wars. Since 1950 European countries have tried to work together.

490 BC Battle of Marathon – a Greek victory against the Persians which opened the greatest age of Greece and saw the birth of democracy and European civilization.

5 BC Birth of Jesus of Nazareth, founder of the Christian religion.

117 AD Roman Empire at its height.

410 Sack of Rome by Alaric the Goth followed by waves of barbarian invasions.

793 onward: Viking raids on Europe including Seville (844).

800 Charlemagne crowned emperor.

1066-1100 Norman conquest of Britain, Italy and Sicily.

1215 Magna Carta, signed by English King John at Runymede sets out legal limits to the power of the monarch for the first time.

1264 First Oxford College founded by Walter de Merton. By 1400 there would be 53 European universities.

1450-55 Gutenburg invents printing. First bible printed.

1453 Constantinople falls to the Turks dispersing scholars and classical learning to the West. Beginning of the Renaissance.

1492 Reconquest of Spain by Ferdinand and Isabella from the Arabs when Granada, the last Islamic city, fell to them; Christopher Columbus sets sail for the New World and discovers the Americas.

1517 Luther initiates the Reformation by publicly protesting against the system of purchasing indulgences.

1519-1522 Ferdinand Magellan circumnavigates the globe.

1536-39 Dissolution of the monasteries by English King Henry VIII.

1648 The Treaty of Westphalia signals the end of the Thirty Years' War.

1643-1715 Louis XIV is king of France.

1789 The French Revolution is followed by the Terror and civil war.

1848 Revolutions in France, Italy, Germany, Hungary and Bohemia.

1870-71 Franco-Prussian war.

1914-18 World War I.

1939-45 World War II.

1951 European Coal and Steel Community formed (Treaty of Paris).

1957 Treaties of Rome create the European Economic Community and Euratom.

1962 Common Agricultural Policy agreed.

1963 First Yaoundé Convention with 17 African countries.

1963 Turkey becomes an associate member of the EC.

1969 Second Yaoundé Convention.

1972 United Kingdom, Ireland and Denmark join the original six.

1975 First Lomé Convention with 46 ACP countries.

1979 First direct elections to European Parliament; creation of European Monetary System; second Lomé Convention with 66 ACP countries.

1981 Greece joins. Ecu formally adopted as European unit of account.

1984 Second direct elections to European Parliament.

1986 Spain and Portugal join; first European passports issued; signing of the Single European Act.

1989 Communist governments fall in Poland, Hungary, East Germany, Czechoslovakia, Bulgaria and Romania.

Glossary

Autonomy is when a person or body is independent and not subject to interference from outside.

Capitalism is the economic system in which most enterprises are owned privately. Wealth or capital can be put to whatever use the individual wants.

Catholic is short for Roman Catholic and is the part of the Christian church headed by the Pope in Rome.

Christianity is the religion started by Jesus of Nazareth. Members of the Christian church believe that Jesus was the son of God.

Communism is the belief that all private wealth should be abolished and all things are held in common, that is, by the state. In practice, the state decides who has money and fixes prices.

Democracy is the system of government where the people regularly elect representatives in a secret ballot from among several political parties.

Ecu stands for economic currency unit. Its value is fixed in relation to a basket of set amounts of other community currencies.

EMS stands for European Monetary System. It came into existence on March 12, 1979. The ecu is the central element of the EMS. Not all EC countries participate fully in the EMS. Greece, Spain, Portugal and the United Kingdom do not.

ERM stands for Exchange Rate Mechanism. It is designed to help European trade by getting rid of extreme changes in the exchange rate of currencies. Central banks agree to support a currency which is in trouble.

European Commission has 17 members and proposes community laws to the Council of Ministers. It supervises the day-to-day running of those policies.

European Parliament Every five years EC electors choose their Members of the European Parliament (MEPs). The parliament has 518 members with a secretariat in Luxembourg. It sits in Strasbourg and has committee meetings in Brussels.

NATO is the North Atlantic Treaty Organization, founded in 1949. It is an alliance between 16 democracies: Belgium, Canada, Denmark, Federal Republic of Germany, France, Greece, Iceland, Italy, Luxembourg, the Netherlands, Norway, Portugal, Spain, Turkey, United Kingdom and the United States.

Nationalism is the enthusiasm for one's country or nation. It became a factor in world politics from 1500 onward.

Parliament is the body of elected representatives, which meets to propose and discuss new laws, agree on taxes and govern a country.

Protestantism is the movement of Christians who broke away from the Roman Catholic church in the 16th century.

Single European Act was signed by the 12 in 1986. It agreed to achieve an open market without barriers within the community by 1992.

Treaties of Rome established the European Economic Community (EEC) and the European Atomic Energy Community (Euratom). They were signed in March 1957 by the Six – France, Federal Republic of Germany, Italy, Belgium, the Netherlands and Luxembourg.

Warsaw Pact is a defense treaty agreeing to mutual military assistance, signed by the Soviet Union, Poland, Czechoslovakia the German Democratic Republic, Hungary Romania and Bulgaria.

World War I was fought from 1914-18. It was the first of two great European wars in the 20th century. The Allies (Britain, France, Russia and later Italy and the United States) fought the Central Powers (Germany, the Austro-Hungarian Empire joined by Turkey). The Allies won and it resulted in the setting up of many smaller nation states in central and eastern Europe.

World War II lasted from 1939-45. It was fought between the Axis powers (Germany, Italy and Japan) and the Allies (the United States, the Soviet Union, Britain, France and others). It ended with the defeat of Japan and Germany and the division of Europe.

Index

1992 3, 20, 27, 32

absolutism 9, 10
ACP countries 25
Africa 8, 25
agriculture 3, 18, 21, 28, 30, 33
associate status 18, 25
Atlantic Alliance 17
atomic bomb 13
Austria 11, 24
Azerbaijanis 23

Belgium 3, 16, 21, 28
Berlin Wall 16
British Commonwealth 17, 32
broadcasting 20, 33
Brussels 28, 32, 33
Bush, George 26

Canada 14
capitalism 3, 4, 35
Caribbean 8, 25
Catholic workers' party 23
Channel Tunnel 24
Charlemagne 6
China 8, 14, 27
Christianity 4-7, 9, 11, 35
Churchill, Winston 16
Cold War 13, 16
colonialism 9-11, 25, 27
Columbus, Christopher 8, 9
Common Agricultural Policy (CAP) 18, 33
Common European bank 19, 27
Common Fisheries Policy 33
communism 11, 13, 16, 22, 23, 26, 27, 35
competition 18, 20
cooperation procedure 20, 32
Council of Ministers 3, 17, 19, 20, 32, 33, 35
Court of Auditors 33
Court of Justice 17, 33
Czechoslovakia 23

De Gaulle, General Charles 18, 19
defense 16, 17, 26
Delors, Jacques 27, 32, 33
democracy 3-5, 7, 10, 13, 15, 19, 22, 23, 28, 35
Denmark 3, 18, 19, 21, 28, 30
direct elections 19, 32, 33

East Germany 13, 16, 22
eastern Europe 11, 13, 16, 22, 23, 26, 27, 30
economic aid 23, 25, 26, 31
Economic and Social Committee 33
economic integration 17, 18, 24
economy 30, 31
ecus 19, 20, 30, 35
Einstein, Albert 10
empires 4, 11, 12, 17, 31
energy 19, 30
Ethiopia 25
European Agricultural Guidance and Guarantee Fund 33
European Atomic Energy Committee (Euratom) 17, 35
European Coal and Steel Community (ECSC) 14, 15, 16, 17
European Commission 17, 20, 21, 27, 28, 32, 33, 35
European Community 2-4, 13, 15, 19, 24, 27, 28
European Constitution 33
European Economic Community (EEC) 17, 18, 19, 35
European Investment Bank 23, 33
European Monetary System (EMS) 19, 35
European Parliament 3, 17, 19-21, 32, 33, 35
European Space Agency 33
Exchange Rate Mechanism (ERM) 19, 35

feudal system 7, 10
France 3, 5-7, 9-12, 14-19, 21, 22, 24, 27, 29, 30
French Revolution 10

German Democratic Republic 16, 29
Germany 2, 3, 5-7, 11-16, 18, 21, 22, 26, 27, 29, 30
Gonzales, Felipe 19
Gorbachev, Mikhail 22, 26

Greece 3-5, 18, 19, 21, 29, 30
guaranteed prices 18, 25, 30, 33

harmonization 18, 33
Honecker, Erich 22
humanism 4, 9
Hungary 16, 23

immigration 27
industrial revolution 10
industry 3, 20, 21, 30, 31
Ireland 3, 18, 19, 21, 29, 32
Islam 7, 9
Israel 25
Italy 3, 5, 7, 11, 12, 16, 17, 20, 21, 29, 30, 32

Japan 30, 33
Joan of Arc 7

Krenz, Egon 22

language 3, 28, 29
law 5, 20, 32, 33
League of Nations 14
Lomé Conventions 25
Luxembourg 3, 14, 16, 21, 29, 30, 32, 33

markets 18, 24, 25
Marx, Karl 10, 11, 35
Members of the European Parliament (MEPs) 19, 35
Middle Ages 7
monetary union 27
Monnet, Jean 13-16
Morocco 25, 27

nation states 7, 11
national security 26
nationalism 12, 24, 35
Netherlands 3, 9, 16, 21, 29, 32, 33
North Atlantic Treaty Organization (NATO) 17, 26, 35

Pétain, Marshal Henri Philippe 14
Poland 13, 14, 16, 23, 27
political union 18, 19, 24, 27
pollution 27
Pompidou, Georges 18
population 3, 25, 28

Portugal 3, 8, 19, 21, 29, 30
printing 8, 9
Protestants 9, 35

raw materials 10, 11, 25, 31
Reformation 4, 9
refugees 16, 27
Regional Development Fund 33
religion 4-7, 9, 29, 35
Renaissance 4, 8, 38
Roman Catholics 9, 35
Rome 4-6, 9, 10
Russian Revolution 11

Schuman, Robert 16
Single European Act 20, 35
single market 3, 20, 24, 26
"Social Charter" 33
Social Fund 33
Solidarnosc (Solidarity) 23
sovereignty 14, 16, 27
Soviet Union 3, 6, 11, 13, 16, 17, 22-24
Spain 3, 5, 7, 9, 19, 21, 29, 30
surpluses 30, 33
Sweden 14, 24
Switzerland 24

technology 4, 10, 27
Third World 25, 31
tourism 27, 31
trade 3, 7, 18, 19, 24, 31, 35
transport 18, 24, 31
Treaties of Rome 17, 18, 26, 27, 35
Turkey 18, 25, 27

United Kingdom 3, 6, 7, 9-12, 14, 16-19, 21, 24, 26, 27, 29
United Nations 32
United States 3, 10, 12-14, 16, 17, 24, 26, 30, 33
United States of Europe 15, 16, 27

Warsaw Pact 17, 35
western civilization 4-6, 9, 11
World War I 11, 12, 14, 16, 35
World War II 2, 12-14, 16, 22, 26, 30, 35

Photographic Credits:
Intro pages and pages 7, 16-17, 21 and 31: J. Allan Cash Library; page 4-5: Werner Forman Archive; page 4-5: Don Slater; pages 6, 8 top and bottom and 10: Mary Evans Picture Library; pages 8 middle, 17, 18, 18-19, 19, 20-21, 22 bottom, 23 bottom, 24 bottom, 26-27, 27 bottom and back cover: Topham Picture Library; page 9: Robert Harding Library; page 12 top: Hulton Picture Company; pages 12 bottom and 13 both: Popperfoto: Page 16: Monnet Archive; page 24-25: Hutchison Library.